Searchlight BOOKS™

World Traveler

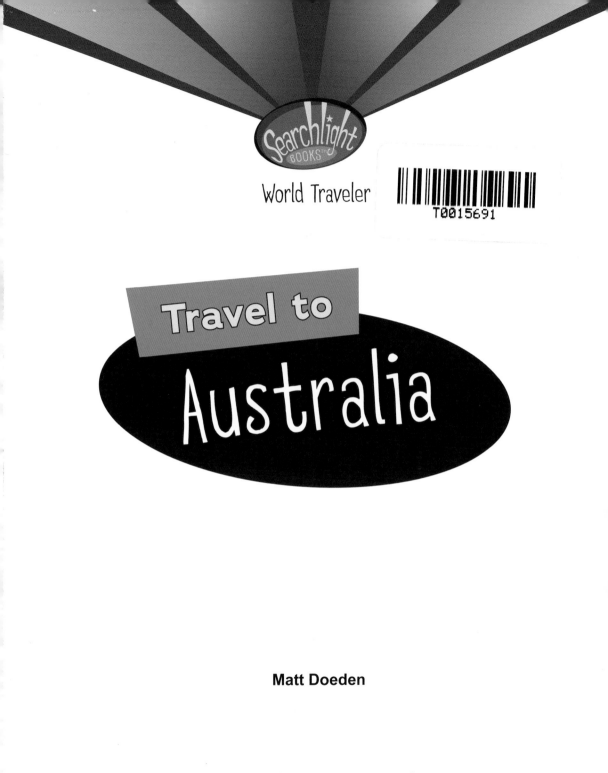

T0015691

Travel to Australia

Matt Doeden

Lerner Publications ◆ Minneapolis

Content consultant: Jon Callow, senior lecturer—language, literacy, and digital media, University of Sydney

Lerner Publications Company
An imprint of Lerner Publishing Group, Inc.
241 First Avenue North
Minneapolis, MN 55401 USA

For reading levels and more information, look up this title
at www.lernerbooks.com.

Main body text set in Adrianna Regular.
Typeface provided by Chank.

Library of Congress Cataloging-in-Publication Data

Names: Doeden, Matt, author.
Title: Travel to Australia / Matt Doeden.
Description: Minneapolis: Lerner Publications, [2022] | Series: Searchlight books—
    world traveler | Includes bibliographical references and index. | Audience: Ages
    8–11 | Audience: Grades 4–6 | Summary: "The land down under boasts fascinating
    geography, landscapes, and cultures. Investigate Australia, from its government and
    history to what life there is like today"—Provided by publisher.
Identifiers: LCCN 2021025144 (print) | LCCN 2021025145 (ebook) | ISBN 9781728441672
    (lib. bdg) | ISBN 9781728448794 (pbk.) | ISBN 9781728444970 (eb pdf)
Subjects: LCSH: Australia—Juvenile literature.
Classification: LCC DU96 .D64 2022 (print) | LCC DU96 (ebook) | DDC 994—dc23

LC record available at https://lccn.loc.gov/2021025144
LC ebook record available at https://lccn.loc.gov/2021025145

Manufactured in the United States of America
1-49922-49765-8/26/2021

Table of Contents

Chapter 1

GEOGRAPHY AND CLIMATE

Australia is an ancient and beautiful land. The nation features rugged mountains, long coastlines, lush forests, and vast deserts.

The Great Barrier Reef stretches more than 1,400 miles (2,300 km) off the coast of northeastern Australia. It is home to corals, fish, and other wildlife. Australia also includes Tasmania, an island off the southeastern coast.

The Land

Australia is both a country and a continent. It is also an island, since it is completely surrounded by water. Australia covers 2,988,902 square miles (7,741,220 sq. km). It is the world's sixth-largest country.

Limestone formations along the southern Australia coast

Australia's most famous animal is the kangaroo.

Four main regions make up Australia. The Coastal Plains lie along eastern Australia. These flat lowlands are home to much of Australia's wildlife and most of its people. Kangaroos, wombats, and platypuses are among the many animals that live on the Coastal Plains.

The Eastern Highlands are west of the Coastal Plains. These mountains are also called the Great Dividing Range because they separate the Coastal Plains from the rest of Australia.

The Central Lowlands stretch across much of central Australia. This flat, low-lying region is mostly covered by desert.

Western Australia is covered by the Western Plateau. This land is also mostly flat, with both deserts and grasslands.

DESERTS COVER VAST AREAS OF CENTRAL AUSTRALIA.

Mountains

Mountains cover many parts of Australia. At 7,310 feet (2,228 m), Mount Kosciuszko is Australia's highest peak. It is in the Snowy Mountains in the Great Dividing Range.

The Stirling Range stands in southwestern Australia. It is home to a huge variety of wildflowers. The Musgrave Ranges and MacDonnell Ranges rise out of the deserts of north-central Australia.

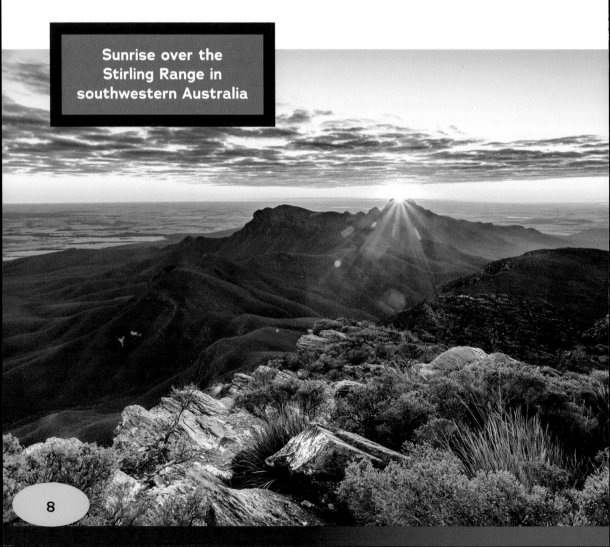

Sunrise over the Stirling Range in southwestern Australia

Must-See Stop:
Uluru-Kata Tjuta National Park

Australia's Northern Territory is home to beautiful Uluru-Kata Tjuta National Park. Uluru is the park's most famous feature. This giant island of sandstone rises out of the desert. Other attractions include the dome-shaped rocks of Kata Tjuta. Visitors can also see ancient rock art here. The pictures and symbols were painted on the rocks thousands of years ago by Aboriginal Australians.

The Murray River meanders through South Australia.

Rivers and Lakes

Some Australian rivers flow into the Pacific Ocean or the Indian Ocean. The Murray is Australia's longest river. It winds about 1,500 miles (2,414 km) from the Eastern Highlands to southern Australia. The Murray empties into the Southern Ocean. Some Australian rivers flow inland into low-lying saltwater lakes. Others dry out as they run through desert lands.

Kati Thanda-Lake Eyre is Australia's biggest lake. This saltwater lake covers 3,668 square miles (9,500 sq. km) in south-central Australia. The lake rises and falls with the weather. After heavy rains, it fills with water. But sometimes it is completely dry.

Climate

Australia has a varied climate. Northern Australia is hot and rainy in the summer, and warm and dry in the winter. Southern Australia has warm summers and much cooler winters. Snow falls in mountainous areas in winter.

Much of western and central Australia is arid. Very little rain falls there. The sun bakes the desert rock, and temperatures can reach 122°F (50°C).

Chapter 2

HISTORY AND GOVERNMENT

People have lived in Australia for at least fifty thousand years. The first inhabitants, Aboriginal Australians, came from islands north and west of Australia. They traveled by boat to the Australian mainland. Another early group settled islands in the Torres Strait, which separates Australia from the islands of New Guinea. The Aboriginal people and the Torres Strait Islanders are known as Indigenous Australians.

New Arrivals

In the 1400s, European explorers began to travel the world's oceans. Dutch explorer Willem Janszoon is the first European known to reach Australia. He arrived in 1606. That year, Spanish explorer Luis Vaez de Torres landed on the continent. English sea captain James Cook explored the eastern coast of Australia in 1770. He claimed the land for Great Britain.

Many Australian settlers arrived as convicts. They lived in prisons like this one in Western Australia.

The British used Australia as a penal colony. The first prisoners arrived in 1788. Free British settlers also came to Australia. The newcomers took land from Indigenous Australians and slayed many of them. The British also brought diseases that killed countless Indigenous people.

A New Nation

In 1901, colonists formed a new nation, the Commonwealth of Australia. Australia fought alongside Britain, the United States, and their allies in World War I (1914–1918) and

World War II (1939–1945). In the late twentieth century, Australia grew rapidly. Industries such as mining and agriculture helped build a strong economy.

Australia is divided into six states and two territories. It has a democratic government. People vote for their leaders.

The federal government has three branches. Parliament, the legislative branch, makes the nation's laws. It has two houses, the Senate and the House of Representatives. The governor-general and the prime minister lead the executive branch, which carries out the laws. The judicial branch ensures laws are carried out fairly.

Australia's legislature meets in this building in Canberra.

Let's Celebrate:
The AFL Grand Final

Australian rules football combines elements of soccer, rugby, and American football. Every September, people flock to Melbourne to watch the Australian Football League (AFL) Grand Final. This game determines the league champions. One of the highlights of the event is the Grand Final parade. There, fans cheer their favorite players as they roll through the streets on pickup trucks.

Chapter 3

CULTURE
AND PEOPLE

Australia is a diverse nation. It has welcomed immigrants
from all around the world. People of European heritage
make up most of the population. They include people of
English, Irish, Scottish, and Dutch descent. Many others
have come to Australia from China, Southeast Asia, India,
and the Middle East. About 3 percent of Australians have
Indigenous roots.

Aboriginal dancers carry on ancient traditions.

Religion

Aboriginal Australians practice an ancient religion. It includes the Dreamtime. In Aboriginal belief, this was the beginning of the world, when all the plants, animals, and places on Earth were created.

Australians of European descent mostly practice Christianity. It is the most widespread religion in Australia. Other religious groups include Muslims (2.6 percent), Buddhists (2.4 percent), and Hindus (1.9 percent). About 30 percent of Australians do not belong to any religious group.

Language and Writing

Australia has no official language. But English is by far the most commonly spoken. About 73 percent of Australians speak English as their main language. Other common languages include Mandarin (a Chinese language) and Arabic.

Before Europeans arrived, Indigenous Australians spoke hundreds of different languages. Most of them

A street sign in Brisbane is written in English and four other languages.

have died out, but a few are still spoken. Many people also speak Aboriginal English. This language blends elements of English and Indigenous languages.

Food and Art

Australian food is a blend of cultures. Traditional English food such as fish and chips crosses paths with spicy sauces from Southeast Asia. Australia's wildlife provides more unique flavors. Favorites include smoked emu, a type of bird, and crocodile meat. Some people try witchetty grubs. These wormlike bugs, which are eaten live, have a nutty flavor.

Dishes made with lamb are popular in Australia.

A gallery in Queensland shows works by Aboriginal artists.

Australia's art draws on its citizens' diverse background. Many Indigenous Australians carry on the artistic traditions of their ancestors. They make wood and rock carvings, and paintings on rock and bark. The nation's many art museums, including the National Gallery of Australia, show off traditional and modern styles.

Must-See Stop:
Sydney Opera House

No trip to Australia is complete without a visit to the Sydney Opera House. One of the world's most famous buildings, it sits on a point in Sydney's harbor. The building's roof looks like a series of sail-shaped shells. Visitors can take in the building's beauty from outside before heading inside to enjoy an opera, musical concert, or play.

Chapter 4

MODERN LIFE

Modern Australia is home to more than twenty-five million people. More than 86 percent of them live in urban areas. Sydney, Melbourne, and Brisbane are the largest cities in Australia. Most of Australia's people live on the Coastal Plains. Much of central and western Australia is very lightly populated.

Australia has a strong economy. Mining, agriculture, and banking are among its biggest industries. Its major crops include wheat, barley, and canola. Many farmers raise sheep for meat and wool.

Many Australians love the outdoors. Some enjoy hiking and rock climbing in the country's remote areas, called the bush or the outback. Others like swimming, snorkeling, boating, and surfing at ocean beaches.

RIDING A WAVE AT MAIN BEACH IN QUEENSLAND
▼

Let's Celebrate:
Barunga Festival

Each June, the small village of Barunga in Australia's Northern Territory hosts a festival of Aboriginal culture. Thousands of people visit to enjoy Aboriginal music, dancing, and food. They can learn about Aboriginal cooking styles, shop for traditional art and crafts, and even learn to make a didgeridoo, a bamboo or wooden trumpet.

Future Challenges

Australia faces big challenges in the future. Global climate change is one concern. Burning fossil fuels releases heat-trapping gases into the air, so temperatures on Earth are rising. The extra heat is also melting ice at the North and South Poles, causing sea levels to rise.

Rising global temperatures have brought record high heat to Australia. High heat and dry conditions have sparked huge wildfires. This problem could grow worse in the future.

Most of Australia's big cities are on the coast. Rising sea levels may cause flooding there.

Because of climate change, some Australian rivers are drying up.

Wind turbines near Melbourne generate clean energy.

Australia is working with other countries to slow climate change. Australians are using more Earth-friendly fuels, such as wind and solar power. Australians hope that taking action will help preserve their land for generations to come.

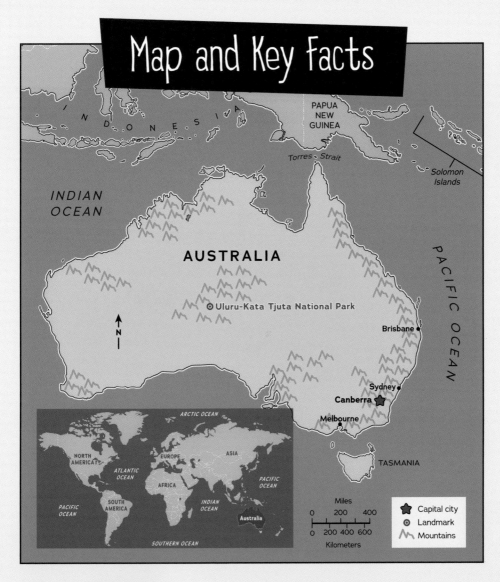

Map and Key Facts

PAPUA NEW GUINEA

INDONESIA

Torres Strait

Solomon Islands

INDIAN OCEAN

AUSTRALIA

PACIFIC OCEAN

○ Uluru-Kata Tjuta National Park

↑ N

Brisbane •

Sydney •

Canberra ⭐

Melbourne

ARCTIC OCEAN

NORTH AMERICA

EUROPE

ASIA

ATLANTIC OCEAN

AFRICA

PACIFIC OCEAN

PACIFIC OCEAN

SOUTH AMERICA

INDIAN OCEAN

Australia

SOUTHERN OCEAN

TASMANIA

Miles
0   200   400

0   200 400 600
Kilometers

⭐ Capital city
◎ Landmark
⋀⋀ Mountains

Flag of Australia

- Continent: Australia
- Capital city: Canberra
- Population: 25 million
- Languages: English, Mandarin, Arabic, and Indigenous languages

Glossary

arid: having little or no rain

climate change: changing weather patterns on Earth caused by the burning of fossil fuels

coral: a sea animal whose skeleton turns into a limestone formation called a coral reef

fossil fuel: coal, oil, and natural gas

Indigenous people: the first people to live in a specific region

penal colony: a settlement where a country sends prisoners

plateau: an area of high, mostly flat land

solar power: energy from the sun

Learn More

Australia Facts for Kids
    https://www.kids-world-travel-guide.com/australia-facts.html

Everett, Reese. *Australia.* North Mankato, MN: Rourke Educational Media, 2019.

Kortemeier, Todd. *Explore Australia: 12 Key Facts.* Mankato, MN: 12 Story Library, 2019.

Morganelli, Adrianna. *Pathways through Australia.* New York: Crabtree, 2020.

National Geographic Kids: Australia
    https://kids.nationalgeographic.com/geography/countries/article/australia

Travel Australia
    https://www.australia.com/en-us

Index

Photo Acknowledgments

Image credits: Luster Designs/Shutterstock.com, p. 5; anek.soowannaphoom/Shutterstock.com, p. 6; ChameleonsEye/Shutterstock.com, pp. 7, 24; bmphotographer/Shutterstock.com, p. 8; eo Tang/Shutterstock.com, p. 9; Ignacio Palacios/Stone/Getty Images, p. 10; EcoPrint/Shutterstock.com, p. 13; Benny Marty/Shutterstock.com, p. 14; Taras Vyshnya/Shutterstock.com, p. 15; Michael Willson/AFL Photos/Getty Images, p. 16; Horizon International Images Limited/Alamy Stock Photo/Alamy Stock Photo, p. 18; richard sowersby/Alamy Stock Photo, p. 19; James de Wall/Moment/Getty Images, p. 20; Travelscape Images/Alamy Stock Photo, p. 21; Irina Sokolovskaya/Shutterstock.com, p. 22; Glenn Campbell/The Sydney Morning Herald/Fairfax Media/Getty Images, p. 24; John Carnemolla/Shutterstock.com, pp. 26–27; Tsvi Braverman/EyeEm/Getty Images, p. 28; Laura Westlund/Independent Picture Service, p. 29.

Cover: swissmediavision/Getty Images.